PRAY-ER

Lenise,

Spend time with the Father!

Gracie O.

PRAY-ER

Starting and Strengthening
Conversations with God

Tracie E. Morrison

Published by Mynd Matters Publishing
715 Peachtree Street NE
Suites 100 & 200
Atlanta, GA 30308
www.myndmatterspublishing.com

ISBN-13: 978-1-953307-78-1

Author photo credit: Tamara Fleming Photography

FIRST EDITION

From their bended knees…

Shirley Plant (Sunshine)
Lorraine Taylor (Aunt Jewel)
Lucille Moore (Ma Moore)
Elder Lisa Barber

…whose shoulders I now stand!

CONTENTS

PROLOGUE

On December 17, 1998, I submitted the final research paper for my Black Religion course entitled, "It's Praying Time." It amazes me that in 2021, the contents within the paper are still relevant today. Here is a summary of my introduction and conclusion:

Prayer is said to "change things." Songs have been written about the power of prayer. The Bible gives us examples of prayers prayed by the apostles, disciples, followers of Jesus and Jesus himself. While the preacher/pastor/clergy/evangelist, may lead and encourage members of the congregation to pray, prayer is an action that can be, and is performed by, numerous lay persons from all denominations, all across the world.

Yet, what exactly is this phenomenon called prayer? How does it work? Why are so many people doing it? Does it *really* change things or is it all part of our imagination? Can anyone pray or is it restricted to religious folks? How do you know what to say – who are you saying it to? How do you know that it is being heard, and will it be answered and by whom?

* * *

Prayer is a personal act of worship—a dialogue—between God and the pray-*er*. It is communication between the pray-*er* and God. Within prayer we are able to ask God for anything. Yet sometimes we abuse our privilege and then question the validity of prayer and God's power within it. Although there is no specific form in which we must pray to God, we must be honest with Him. We must remember that He wants us to ask Him anything in His name. In our asking though, we must maintain the image of God as Holy and Omnipresent, everywhere at the same time. It matters not whether we pray corporately or privately. But it does matter when we do not pray.

Prayer *does* change things. Although there are times when we cannot have some things when we want them, God is always on time. So, we must be patient in our prayers. Faith is the key to prayer and honesty unlocks our blessings. In today's society, with everything that is happening, *it's always prayer time.*

INTRODUCTION

Have you ever been overwhelmed by other people's expectations, criticisms and standards? Since I was a teenager, I desperately wanted to be accepted, to fit in and to belong. I valued the opinions of others so much that I would morph into who they wanted me to become or who they needed me to be for them. When those relationships ended, I was left feeling empty, abandoned, and rejected. It was in those moments that I learned to pray.

In prayer, I found a safe, judgement-free zone where I could just be…unapologetically me. Flawed me. Imperfect me. God, more than anyone else, accepted me for who I was. The more I spent time getting to know Him through prayer, the more He revealed about Himself and who I was as His child.

In the beginning stages of my prayer life, I did most of the talking or emoting about the way other people treated me. Had I not helped them achieve their goals, listened to their problems, and supported them in their time of need? It wasn't fair! *God, why? I don't understand.* God did not always respond to my questions or respond in a manner that I felt was acceptable. So, I would throw adult-sized temper tantrums—folding my arms, screaming toward the ceiling, crying into my mattress, or giving Him the silent treatment. There was no way I was going to talk to Him or carry out His will if I wasn't going to get my way.

One day in prayer, God showed me a running track. There was a runner in each lane holding a baton. When the race started, I would leave my lane and go run along aside another runner, cheering them on and even offering to carry their baton to the finish line. Once we reached the finish line, the runner would relish in their win. I may or may not receive any acknowledgement or gratitude. Yet, I kept running alongside others, helping them carry their baton to the finish line. When they had all finished running their races, I returned to the starting line of my own lane, but I was too tired to run the race. At that moment, God said, "Stay in your lane. Run the race that I have given to you." I had frustrated myself. It wasn't God's fault. I was so *busy* running, I never had time to hear God's voice.

The Scripture tells us in John 10:27, *"My own sheep will hear my voice and I know each one, and they will follow me." The Passion Translation (TPT)*

Here's how I interpreted what God was saying:
- *"My own* sheep" → I *belong* to God.
- *"Hear* my voice"→ I will know God's voice when He speaks.

- I know *each* one → God knows my unique voice.
- They will *follow* me → I follow God because I belong to Him.

In order to run and finish my race, I needed to hear God's voice above the noise of the world and the chatter of competing voices, including the voices of those who were well-meaning, those that meant me harm, and even my own voice. Understanding this, I began to pray:

Father, tune my ears to hear your voice ever so clearly. Help me hear the very words that fall from your lips. Help me hear your heart. When you speak, help me Lord, to obey! May I complete every Divine Assignment in a spirit of efficiency and excellence! May I arrive at every Divine Appointment in time and on time! May I make every Divine Connection! Help me not to run ahead of you or fall behind out of fear. Grant me wisdom, knowledge, and keenly-sharp discernment! Open the eyes of my understanding and grant me crystal clear clarity in this season, in Jesus' name I pray, Amen!

This book is a compilation of the prayer exercises I have shared during weekly prayer service, in workshop sessions, and the prayers I have prayed for myself and others over the last twenty plus years. Developing a relationship with God through prayer is simply one little talk with Jesus at a time. As you journey through the exercises and activities, take your time. There is no rush. Enjoy getting to know God and you better!

Have a little talk with Jesus. Tell Him all about your troubles.

He will hear your faintest cry…Answer by and by. Feel the little prayer wheels turning; know that the fire is burning. Just a little talk with Jesus makes it right!

—Cleavant Derricks, 1937

THE INVITATION

Like most children who attend Sunday School and Vacation Bible School, I had to memorize and/or recite The Lord's Prayer, Psalm 23, The Apostle's Creed, Ten Commandments, and John 3:16. Moving from rote memory and recitation to having a relationship with Jesus Christ takes work, courage, reflection, and at times, isolation.

If you don't already have a relationship with Jesus Christ, it is my sincere prayer that you will accept Him into your heart TODAY! This is one of the most important prayers you will pray. Allow me to extend the invitation.

Pray this prayer aloud:
> *Lord, I **recognize** I need you in my life.*
> *I **repent** of any wrongdoings.*
> *I **request** you make my heart your home.*
> *I look forward to having a **relationship** with you,*
> *In Jesus' name! Amen!*

God loves you! More than anything, He wants to be in a relationship with you. It may be awkward at first and it's okay. Keep showing up. Hang in there during the good and bad moments of your life. Don't give up! Even if you do, know that God will be right there waiting to pick things up exactly where you left off.

Trust and believe that God is committed to developing a long-term relationship with you through prayer.

If you have been dating God on and off, I hope this book will encourage you to take a leap of faith and make a strong commitment to wholeheartedly serving God. Whether you have been walking with God for a little or a long time, these words are meant to strengthen the bond you already have with God and to help you tap into new areas of power, authority, and anointing as you continue along the journey.

No matter where you are on the prayer continuum, make a commitment to tune your ears to hear God's voice!

LET US PRAY

Our Father and our God, we come ready to surrender.
Search us. Leave nothing within us untouched by you.
We give you our minds. Help us think on those things that are lovely, that are pure, that are honest, just, and of good report.
We give you our eyes. Help us see ourselves as you see us, O God, as children of purpose and promise.
We give you our ears. Tune our ears to hear your voice, then help us God to obey.
We give you our noses. We want to smell and bask in the sweet aroma of your presence. Teach us how to linger in your presence God.
We give you our lips. Season our words with grace. May the words we speak reflect the love and mercy you show us daily.
We give you our shoulders. We cast our cares on you, and we lay aside every weight and the sin that so easily ensnares us.
We give you our arms. Help us lift them in adoration, praise, and worship unto you.
We give you our hands. Wash our hands God. We want them to be clean and fit for service unto you. Help us to be about our Father's business, busy doing the work of the kingdom.

We give you our hearts. Create within us clean hearts and renew within us a right spirit, a willing heart to serve, a pure heart to worship, an open heart to receive your instruction.
We give you our lungs. Breathe new life in us.
We give you our knees. Teach us how to bend our knees in prayer and reverence to you.
We give you our legs. May we stand like trees planted by the river, rooted and grounded in you.
Lastly God, we give you our feet. Order our steps according to your will and your word.
Holy Spirit be our companion and our guide.
We surrender ourselves to you in Jesus' name.
Amen!

I am praying to you because I know you will answer, O God. Bend down and listen as I pray.

—Psalms 17:6 NLT

LORD, WHERE DO I BEGIN?

FOLLOW THE INSTRUCTOR

Guiding Scriptures:

God, the Master, told the dry bones, "Watch this: I'm bringing the breath of life to you and you'll come to life." —Ezekiel 37:5

Come on. Let's go back to God. —Hosea 6:1

If you've ever taken yoga or Tai Chi, there are basic steps that one must follow to get the most out of a session. First, take several deep breaths. Second, set your intention. Lastly, assume the various positions as led by your instructor. Now the general purpose of participating in yoga or Tai Chi is to relax, to stretch, and while entering into various poses, to breathe, which then allows the mind, body, and spirit of the participant to be restored. While this may not be a yoga or Tai Chi class, I would like to walk you through some basic steps as you begin your prayer journey.

STEP 1: TAKE A DEEP BREATH

In Genesis 2:7, the Bible tell us: "And the Lord formed man of the dust of the ground, and breathed into his nostrils the breath of life; and man became a living being." Our ability to breathe is a clear indicator of our God-given life and existence in the world.

Taking a deep breath requires you to inhale through your nose, filling your belly full of air and then exhaling, gently and slowly, releasing a stream of air through your mouth. As you inhale, imagine God breathing into your nostrils filling your belly with His spirit. As you exhale, take notice of the dry and dormant places that need to be revived and brought back to life in this season. Each time you inhale, focus on that dry place. It is in that place that God desires to renew your spirit.

Take a moment and practice step one. Once you're comfortable in your seat, take three deep breaths at your own pace. Are you feeling a little more relaxed? Good. Now we'll move on to Step Two.

STEP 2: SET YOUR INTENTION

Hosea beckons us in Chapter 6:1, "Come on, let's go back to God." In the earlier chapters, Hosea tells the people that the land has dried up because of their failure to acknowledge and be faithful to God. He then calls for them to return to God, reminding them that even though they were punished, if they repented, God would still be faithful. He would heal, bind up their wounds, revive and restore them, and they would live in His presence. Has your failure to acknowledge or remain faithful to God cut off your air supply? Just like in Hosea, God is faithful to us. Follow the instructions found in Hosea: "Come on, let's go back to God." Set your heart to repentance and your intentions on the Master, the one who is able to heal, revive, and restore us.

STEP 3: ASSUME THE POSITIONS AS LED BY YOUR INSTRUCTOR

Your position or posture is prayer. Your instructor is God. His heart's desire is to clear away and remove any obstruction that's restricting or cutting off your connection to Him. It does not matter if you are on the novice, intermediate or advanced level in your prayer life. God yearns to breathe fresh air into your situation. He wants to revive that dry place. So, when you pray, don't be in a hurry! Take deep breaths. Fill your nostrils with His breath.

God is breathing new life, new ministry, new purpose, new instructions, new plans, new creativity, and new ideas into your belly. Take deep breaths. Let the air move from the crown of your head down to the soles of your feet. Leave no place void of His life-giving breath. To get the most out of your sessions, be sure to listen for and carefully follow the directions of The Master Instructor—God.

Take your positions…

PRAYER POSTURES

Give I Unto Thee *(Prostrate) Nehemiah 8:6*

Lay face down. Silence the distractions. God is your only audience during this sacred time. Give Him access to your heart and control of you mind. Willingly give Him your thoughts, desires, burdens and pain. Give everything to the Lord! Don't forget when you get up, leave everything you gave Him in His most capable hands.

Worship at His Feet *(Kneeling) Psalm 99:5*

Picture our Heavenly Father seated on His throne. Worship by kneeling at His feet. Imagine God reaching His hand down to touch you in your time of need. Tell God what you need.

Forgive Us As We Forgive *(Standing with Uplifted Hands)* Mark 11:25

Admit you have sinned. *Ask* God to forgive you. *Accept* His forgiveness. Grant *Access* to your prayers by forgiving others who may have wronged you.

Hear My Prayer *(Sitting)* 1 John 5:14-15

When we are confident in prayer, we no longer walk the floors at night. Taking a seat means God can stand in your situation and work it out on your behalf.

He Walks With Me *(Walking)* **John 15:7**

Walk into this new season of your prayer life confidently, boldly, and giving God ALL the praise!

THE LORD'S PRAYER

Prayer is a dialogue or conversation with G... ...t consists of three basic parts:

Part One: Talking to God.

Part Two: Listening to or for God.

Part Three: Reflecting on and recording what God says to us when we pray.

The Lord's Prayer, found in Matthew 6:9-13 (KJV), is the Biblical foundation from which many of us learn to pray. Jesus teaches us how to pray and provides a scaffold for what to include when we pray.

Directions: Read the Scripture and answer the subsequent questions. Use the responses from each question to develop your own prayer.

Scripture: Matthew 6:9-13 (KJV)

"After this manner therefore pray ye:"

"Our Father" Who is God to you? How do you identify yourself in relation to God?

"which art in heaven," In what ways is God's vantage point better than our own?

"Hallowed be thy name." Do you respect God's authority? If so, how? If not, why?

"Thy kingdom come, Thy will be done" What will you have to let go/surrender in order to allow God control over your life?

"in earth, as it is in heaven." What has God assigned you to do here on earth?

"Give us this day our daily bread." What petitions, needs or requests are you bringing to God today?

"And forgive us our debts," What do you need God to pardon on your behalf?

"as we forgive our debtors." Who are the persons you need to pardon?

"And lead us not into temptation," Where are some places you no longer need to go or people you need to release?

"but deliver us from evil," What habits, issues, concerns try to trap you or stunt your Christian growth?

"For thine is the kingdom, and the power, and the glory, forever." What is your understanding of this statement?

"Amen." It is done. In Jesus' name!

5 W'S OF PRAYER

Many of us learned the 5 W's: Who, What, When, Where, Why, in either English Language Arts or Social Studies class. The 5 W's can also serve as a guide to help us strengthen our prayer devotional time:

Directions: On a separate sheet of paper, respond to the following prompts/questions.

I. WHO? *(Who is God to me?)*
Names/Characteristics of God:

_____

_____

_____

_____

_____

II. WHAT? *(What is prayer?)*
Write your own definition:

_____

_____

_____

_____

_____

(What do I say as I pray?)
Brainstorm things you can share with God during prayer from any of the following:

Thanksgiving/Gratitude
Repentance/Forgiveness
Intercession/Petition
Surrender/Letting Go
Other?

_____

_____

_____

_____

_____

_____

III. WHEN? *(When will I pray?)*
Read the following scriptures:
Ephesians 6:18
Luke 18:1
Psalm 5:3
Acts 16:25
1 Thessalonians 5:17
Acts 6:4
Psalm 55:17
Daniel 6:10, 13

What insight did you gain about *when* to pray?

_____

_____

_____

_____

_____

_____

Create a prayer schedule. *(Keep in mind Psalm 121:3-4)*

IV. WHERE? *(Where will I go to pray?)*

Read: *Matthew 6:6*

Journal Exercise:

What do I need to clean out of my (mental, emotional, spiritual) "closet" in order for me to get in, close the door, and meet God? (*1 Peter 5:7*)

_____

_____

_____

_____

_____

_____

_____

V. WHY? *(Why am I praying?)*

Read the following scriptures:
Jabez *(1 Chronicles 4:9-10)*
Children of Israel *(Numbers 14:1-3)*:
God's People *(Joel 2)*:
Jesus *(Luke 23:33-37)*
Woman w/ Issue of Blood *(Matthew 9:19-21)*:
Paul *(Colossians 1:9-12)*
John *(1 John 5:14-15)*
Jude *(Jude 1:24-25)*
Hannah *(1 Samuel:10-16)*

List the needs or reasons mentioned in the scriptures above.

Are the prayer requests similar or different than ours today? How so?

I pray because...

_____

_____

_____

_____

_____

_____

HOW? *(How will I pray?)*

Use one of the postures and positions the Bible offers us to commune with God:

Prayer Position/Posture	Monday	Tuesday	Wednesday	Thursday	Friday	Saturday	Sunday
Walk							
Notes							
Sit							
Notes							
Kneel							
Notes							
Stand							
Notes							
Bow down							
Notes							
Lay prostrate							
Notes							
Clap							
Notes							
Lift/ Wave Hands							
Notes							
Dance							
Notes							
Speak in Tongues/Use Prayer Language							
Notes							
Sing							
Notes							

THE ESSENTIAL TOOLS

Read: Mark 6:3; Ephesians 2:8-10;
James 2:20-22

Jesus was a carpenter. The Bible refers to us as God's workmanship. God holds the blueprint to our lives. When we veer away from the plan, He begins the remodeling process. His toolbox has everything needed to ensure His purpose and plan are manifested in the earth. We have a role and responsibility in the process as well. We must add our faith and action in obedience to what we hear God saying to us in prayer. Be sure to keep these tools handy and refer to them as you build, repair, or remodel your prayer closet.

Hammer – To Build Up and To Demolish
2 Corinthians 4:8-10: We are hard pressed on every side, but not crushed; perplexed, but not in despair, persecuted, but not abandoned; struck down, but not destroyed. We always carry around in our body the death of Jesus, so that the life of Jesus may also be revealed in our body.

Are you able to identify the areas in your life that need to be torn down? Who are the people in your life that help to encourage and build your faith in God?

Tape Measure – To Measure

2 Peter 3:8 (ESV): But do not overlook this one fact, beloved, that with the Lord one day is as a thousand years, and a thousand years as one day.

You are making progress. Celebrate even the tiniest of steps. Count every blessing!

Wrench – To Tighten and To Loosen
Matthew 16:17-19 (MSG): Jesus came back, "God bless you, Simon, son of Jonah! You didn't get that answer out of books or from teachers. My Father in heaven, God himself, let you in on this secret of who I really am. And now I'm going to tell you who you are, really are. You are Peter, a rock. This is the rock on which I will put together my church, a church so expansive with energy that not even the gates of hell will be able to keep it out. ¹⁹ And that's not all. You will have complete and free access to God's kingdom, keys to open any and every door: no more barriers between heaven and earth, earth and heaven. A yes on earth is yes in heaven. A no on earth is no in heaven."

Ultimately, God has the power to open and close doors in your life. He empowers us as we develop an intimate relationship with Him. This is why it is necessary to come to Him in prayer so we may arrive at the appointed doors, receive the keys, enter, and fulfill our Divine assignments.

Are you standing at a door? How do you plan to use the keys God is giving you?

Screwdriver – To Pry, Scrape, Nudge; To Apply Pressure

Luke 22:44 (Good News Translation): Jesus left the city and went, as he usually did, to the Mount of Olives; and the disciples went with him. When he arrived at the place, he said to them, "Pray that you will not fall into temptation."

Then he went off from them about the distance of a stone's throw and knelt down and prayed. "Father," he said, "if you will, take this cup of suffering away from me. Not my will, however, but your will be done." An angel from heaven appeared to him and strengthened him. In great anguish he prayed even more fervently; his sweat was like drops of blood falling to the ground.

There are times in our lives when we are overwhelmed. We cry out to God asking Him to ease the pressure or make the pain stop altogether. God is with us even in our crushing moments.

What suffering are you experiencing right now? Are you ready to let His will be done? What steps are you taking to trust God?

Pliers – To Cut, Bend, Grip

Romans 9:17-21 (NIV): For Scripture says to Pharaoh: "I raised you up for this very purpose, that I might display my power in you and that my name might be proclaimed in all the earth." Therefore, God has mercy on whom he wants to have mercy, and he hardens whom he wants to harden.

One of you will say to me: "Then why does God still blame us? For who is able to resist his will?" But who are you, a human being, to talk back to God? "Shall what is formed say to the one who formed it, 'Why did you make me like this?'" Does not the potter have the right to make out of the same lump of clay some pottery for special purposes and some for common use?"

God's correction is usually painful and unwanted, but it is how Christians grow stronger! Imagine God as your plastic surgeon. Which areas would He mark with an 'x' in preparation for corrective surgery?

Drill – Driving Holes
*John 10:10 (NIV): The thief comes only to **steal** and **kill** and **destroy**; I have come that they may have life, and have it to the full.*

Satan comes to poke holes in our minds, our hearts, our plans and our relationship with God. He delights in stealing joy, killing faith and destroying hope. What tools can you immediately grab to defeat the enemy?

Level – The Straight Line/Balance

Luke 3:4-6: As it is written in the book of the words of Isaiah the prophet: "A voice of one calling in the wilderness, 'Prepare the way for the Lord, make straight paths for him. Every valley shall be filled in, every mountain and hill made low. The crooked roads shall become straight, the rough ways smooth. And all people will see God's salvation.'

The path of life is not in a straight line. Thankfully, God is able to make the crooked places straight and work all things for our good.

What are some best practices in handling life's unexpected turns?

Utility Knife – Super Sharp Blade, to Cut and Scrape

John 15:1-5: "I am the true vine, and my Father is the gardener. He cuts off every branch in me that bears no fruit, while every branch that does bear fruit he prunes so that it will be even more fruitful. You are already clean because of the word I have spoken to you. Remain in me, as I also remain in you. No branch can bear fruit by itself; it must remain in the vine. Neither can you bear fruit unless you remain in me.

I am the vine; you are the branches. If you remain in me and I in you, you will bear much fruit; apart from me you can do nothing."

Cuts hurt! They cause you to bleed and they take time to heal. Depending on how you treat the cut, it may sting or burn. Left untreated, cuts can become infected and lead to more serious problems. Not all moments in prayer will "feel good." It is okay to say, "Ouch." It's okay to cry.

Identify your reaction during God's correction or in moments of conviction. How do you respond when God's answer is wait? Not yet? No?

I DECREE & DECLARE

The Bible declares in Job 22:28 (KJV), *Thou shalt also decree a thing, and it shall be established unto thee: and the light shall shine upon thy ways.*

Directions: Say the following confession aloud.

I Declare:

- That the peace of God will enter into my mind and destroy all confusion sent by the enemy. (Philippians 4:7)

- That the joy of the Lord is my strength. (Nehemiah 8:10)

- That I will use wisdom when making decisions. (Proverbs 4:7)

- That I will gain understanding of my God-ordained assignment. (Psalm 119:104)

- That the plots of the enemy against me are canceled in the name of Jesus Christ. (John 10:10)

- That the blessings of God will overtake me.
  (Deuteronomy 28:1-2)

- That I am a blessing to the nation. (Malachi 3:12)

- That my children are purpose-filled by the Lord.
  (Matthew 21:16)

- That no weapon formed against me will prosper.
  (Isaiah 54:17)

- That the healing hand of God will cancel every
  sickness or disease and replace it with wholeness.
  (Isaiah 53:5)

- That I am no longer a victim but a victor in Jesus'
  name. (I John 4:4)

- That the God who began a good work in me will
  carry it out to completion. (Philippians 1:6)

- That I can do all things through Christ which
  strengthens me. (Philippians 4:13)

- That my God shall supply all of my needs according to His riches in glory. (Philippians 4:19)

- That the lies of man have no power over my life. (Psalm 110:1)

- That the generational curses in my life are broken from my life. (Matthew 11:29)

- That my finances are pressed down, shaken together, and running over with abundance. (Luke 6:38)

- That I am blessed to be a blessing. (Hebrews 6:14)

- That I am fearfully and wonderfully made by the hand of God. (Psalm 139:14)

- That I am FREE to praise the Lord. (Psalm 150:6)

- That I have power and authority through Jesus Christ to bind every demon and ungodly spirit. (Matthew 16:19)

- That I will not fear! (2 Timothy 1:7)

- That I am more than a conqueror and NO-THING can separate me from the love of my Abba! (Romans 8:37-39)

_____

_____(Scripture)

_____

_____(Scripture)

_____

_____(Scripture)

_____

_____(Scripture)

_____

_____(Scripture)

I decree and declare it to be so.
In Jesus' name, AMEN, AMEN, AMEN!

LORD, I AM READY TO PRAY

"Let us then with confidence draw near to the throne of grace, that we may receive mercy and find grace to help in time of need."

—Hebrews 4:16 (ESV)

PRAYER STARTERS

Prayer can sometimes seem overwhelming. There is no right or wrong way to pray. All God desires is a relationship. One of the best ways to develop a relationship is to communicate. Here are a few different ways to initiate or spice up your prayer life. Try something different or new today.

Directions: Using the following prompts, start a prayer by mix-&-matching, journaling, writing, filling in the blank, and praying.

1. Father we
2. God I
3. You are so
4. We bless
5. You are worthy
6. We exalt
7. We lift up
8. As we worship
9. Today we ask
10. God I thank
11. Your presence
12. Speak to
13. There is
14. Our heart
15. Our minds
16. Our souls
17. In this place, we
18. Glory
19. We praise
20. Into your presence
21. We offer
22. Daddy, I come
23. You are
24. Wonderful Counselor
25. Joy
26. We await
27. We expect
28. Our desire
29. Our hope
30. We acknowledge
31. Great Jehovah
32. Savior

33. We bless
34. We honor
35. Sovereign God
36. O, Lord
37. Heal
38. Save
39. We need you
40. Hallelujah
41. You are our
42. Holy Father
43. Lamb of God
44. Jesus, we cry
45. Your name
46. We ask for
47. Thank you for
48. Hear our prayer
49. _____
50. _____
(your own)
(your own)

...in Jesus' name, Amen!

SING HYMNS

Hymns were always part of Sunday service. I fondly remember holding the hymnal and singing them as a child. As an adult, I find myself singing those hymns in my darkest and loneliest moments. They are often the prayers of the author, which is perhaps why they bring me so much comfort. I have listed the stanzas, verses, and refrains for some of the hymns that have brought me through challenging times. It was just Hymn and I in those moments.

Directions: Read (or sing) the lyrics in the hymn and answer the following questions before you pray.

Amazing Grace

1 Amazing grace (how sweet the sound)
that saved a wretch like me!
I once was lost, but now am found,
was blind, but now I see.

2 'Twas grace that taught my heart to fear,
and grace my fears relieved;
how precious did that grace appear
the hour I first believed!

3 Through many dangers, toils and snares
I have already come:

'tis grace has brought me safe thus far,
and grace will lead me home.

4 The Lord has promised good to me,
his word my hope secures;
he will my shield and portion be
as long as life endures.
—John Newton (1779)

Sometimes I have a bad habit of thinking God blesses me only because of good performance. In the moments when I do not perform well or do not perform at all, God continues to extend His grace—unearned, unmerited favor—and unconditional love toward me. No matter the situation, I have learned that God's grace is enough!

How has God's grace been amazing in your life?

Think about all the promises found in God's word. Take a moment to write scriptures that remind you of God's promise(s) to you.

_____

_____

_____

_____

_____

_____

Count Your Blessings

Count your blessings, name them one by one;
Count your blessings, see what God hath done;
Count your blessings, name them one by one;
Count your many blessings, see what God hath
done. —Johnson Oatman (1897)

Directions: Start a gratitude journal. Each day, create a list of things you are grateful or thankful to God for doing in your life.

Journal/Sentence Prompts:
Thank you, Lord for…
Father, I am grateful for…
I give thanks to you because…
Thank you! Amen!

What A Friend We Have in Jesus
What a friend we have in Jesus,
all our sins and griefs to bear!
What a privilege to carry
everything to God in prayer!
O what peace we often forfeit,
O what needless pain we bear,
all because we do not carry
everything to God in prayer!

2Have we trials and temptations?
Is there trouble anywhere?
We should never be discouraged;
take it to the Lord in prayer!
Can we find a friend so faithful,
who will all our sorrows share?
Jesus knows our every weakness;
take it to the Lord in prayer!

3Are we weak and heavy laden,
cumbered with a load of care?
Precious Savior, still our refuge—
take it to the Lord in prayer!
Do your friends despise, forsake you?
Take it to the Lord in prayer!
In his arms he'll take and shield you;
you will find a solace there.
—Joseph Medlicott Scriven (1855)

According to Romans 3:23, we have ALL sinned and fallen short of God's glory. What sins, pain, and sorrow are you currently carrying?

Identify and list the "trouble" in your home, on your job, in your neighborhood, state, or country that you are bringing to God in prayer? In what areas are you overwhelmed and burdened? How can God provide you comfort and solace?

'Tis So Sweet to Trust In Jesus

'Tis so sweet to trust in Jesus,
and to take him at his word;
just to rest upon his promise,
and to know, "Thus saith the Lord."
—Louisa M. R. Stead (1882)

I have often struggled with trusting God and taking Him at His word. Although there are moments when I question Him and what He is doing in my life, I am daily learning to trust Him more. Where are areas in your life that you are learning to trust God or trust God more?

_____

_____

_____

_____

_____

_____

It Is Well

When peace like a river attendeth my way,
when sorrows like sea billows roll;
whatever my lot, thou hast taught me to say,
"It is well, it is well with my soul."
—Horatio Gates Spafford (1873)

Often sung at funerals, it has been standing over my kitchen sink washing dishes, kneeling beside my bed in tears, or sitting in my car that I find myself singing this hymn. When my heart is overwhelmed, and I feel as though I cannot and do not have the strength to continue on, God steps in and reminds me…*It is well. Selah.*

May it be well with your soul, Amen!

Great Is Thy Faithfulness
Refrain:
Great is thy faithfulness!
Great is thy faithfulness!
Morning by morning, new mercies I see.
All I have needed thy hand hath provided.
Great is thy faithfulness, Lord, unto me!

Pardon for sin and a peace that endureth,
thine own dear presence to cheer and to guide,
strength for today and bright hope for tomorrow;
blessings all mine, with ten thousand beside! [Refrain]
—Thomas O. Chisholm (1923)

Do you recognize the faithfulness of God? Even when we turn our back on Him and walk away, He has mercy on us, forgives us, and continues to provide for us.

Directions: Reflect in your journal on the ways God has cheered you up, guided you along the right path, given you strength and hope for the future.

Nothing But the Blood

What can wash away my sin?
Nothing but the blood of Jesus.
What can make me whole again?
Nothing but the blood of Jesus.
Refrain:
O precious is the flow
that makes me white as snow;
no other fount I know;
nothing but the blood of Jesus.
—Robert Lowry (1876)

There's Power In the Blood

Refrain:
There is pow'r, pow'r, wonder-working pow'r
In the blood of the Lamb;
There is pow'r, pow'r, wonder-working pow'r
In the precious blood of the Lamb.
—Lewis E. Jones (1899)

Holy Communion has always been and should always be a sacred space for reflection, remembrance, and repentance. It is a reminder of the sacrifice of God's Son, Jesus Christ, on Calvary for each one of us. His body, broken and bruised, and His blood, draining and dripping.

The Blood of Jesus! It reaches. It washes. It covers. It keeps. It heals. It protects. The Blood has POWER! When we are in right relationship with God, that Blood flows through our veins and washes away sin, brings healing to our mind, body and soul, protects us from the ongoing barrage of attacks from the enemy, and gives us strength to face each day. We cannot afford to forget the tremendous sacrifice Jesus made dying on the cross for *our* sins.

Directions: Remember Jesus Christ's sacrifice on the cross. Be thankful for the benefits of the Blood of Jesus. Plea the blood of Jesus over every area of your life.

Create a list of things you value. Next, list the reason(s) why you value them. How do you treat the things you value?

_____

_____

_____

_____

_____

_____

_____

Do you value the above-mentioned things more than your relationship with Jesus Christ? If so, reflect on why more value is placed in those items? What connects you to the things you value?

_____

_____

_____

_____

_____

_____

_____

How do you recognize and handle attacks from Satan and his army? Who/What do you rely on to protect you when unexpected attacks show up in your life?

In what way are the protections afforded within our culture and society different from the hedge of protection provided by God? Read John 10:28-30.

_____

_____

_____

_____

_____

_____

Read and Reflect on 1 Corinthians 11:23-32 (NKJV).
If God leads you to do so, take Holy Communion.

Blessed Assurance

1 Blessed assurance, Jesus is mine.
Oh, what a foretaste of glory divine.
Heir of salvation, purchase of God,
born of his Spirit, washed in his blood.

Refrain:
This is my story, this is my song,
praising my Savior all the day long.
This is my story, this is my song,
praising my Savior all the day long.

2 Perfect communion, perfect delight,
visions of rapture now burst on my sight.
Angels descending bring from above
echoes of mercy, whispers of love. [Refrain]

3 Perfect submission, all is at rest.
I in my Savior am happy and bless'd,
watching and waiting, looking above,
filled with his goodness, lost in his love.
—Fanny Crosby (1873)

How is God writing your story? What assurances has He provided to you and those you love?

_____

_____

_____

_____

_____

_____

_____

Romans 8:37-39, *Take time to get "lost in His love."*

Just As I Am

Just as I am, without one plea,
but that thy blood was shed for me,
and that thou bidd'st me come to thee,
O Lamb of God, I come, I come.
—Charlotte Elliott (1836)

What is the purpose of filters on social media, Photoshop for pictures, or edits to a document? According to this hymn, how does God want you to show up in prayer?

_____

_____

_____

_____

_____

_____

_____

_____

I Need Thee Every Hour

I need Thee ev'ry hour,
Most gracious Lord;
No tender voice like Thine
Can peace afford.

Refrain:
I need Thee, oh, I need Thee;
Ev'ry hour I need Thee;
Oh, bless me now, my Savior,
I come to Thee.
—Annie S. Hawks (1872); Author (refrain): Robert
Lowry (1872)

I have always been pretty independent and self-reliant. With a Type A personality, for years I struggled with rigidity, perfectionism, and people-pleasing—all of which had a negative impact on my emotional state and mental wellbeing. I have come to learn, however, that I cannot do this thing called life on my own. The moment I came to that realization and admitted that I

NEED God's help, the burdens lifted and I saw things more clearly. Will you admit that you need God, too?

Extended Activity

Research other hymns of the church. Reflect on the lyrics. How do the lyrics bring meaning to your life and situation? Use the hymn as a catalyst for your prayers.

PRAYER OPTIONS

Your prayers do not have to look or sound the same every day. Changing up the routine will help your prayer life remain vibrant. Mix and match any of these prayer forms with others you have already learned or will learn in the future.

Silence
Read: Psalm 62:5-8

Sit quietly. Listen for God. What does God want to say to you? Open your ears and open your heart.

Tongues/Laying on of Hands
Read: Acts 19:4-6

Open your mouth in faith. Trust your spirit to pray in an unknown tongue. God has given you the power to lay hands on yourself and be healed.

Write/Reflect
John 14:25-27

Write a prayer for someone else. Text, email, mail or hand-deliver it. Reflect on who God is to you and all He has done for you.

Praise & Worship
Psalm 150:1-6

Clap your hands. Dance before the Lord. Sing a new song. Leap for joy. Shout unto God with a voice of triumph. PRAISE THE LORD!

Tarry
Habakkuk 2:3
"...Linger, take a long time, (response) slow in coming"

There will be times when you have to tarry at the altar or in your prayer closet until breakthrough, healing, deliverance, strength, peace, joy; until a change in your situation or circumstances; until a change in your heart, your mind, until a change in YOU, occurs!

Partner/Small Group
Matthew 18:20
Schedule time to pray with others. Know that God will be in the midst. Pray for one another and the matters, issues, and situations that God places on your hearts.

Others:

_____

_____

_____

_____

_____

NAMES OF GOD

Praying the names of God helps us to further understand His nature and character. Below you will find some names of God with a short prayer or confession.

Directions: Choose one name of God each day. Say the name aloud. Pray the short prayer, add to it or pray your own prayer. Throughout the day, try to connect how God's name is manifesting itself in your daily routine.

ROCK OF SALVATION
I call upon and lean on you today, God. Thank you for being the foundation of my faith.

MY GLORY
God, you are my glory, and the lifter of my bowed head.

MY FORTRESS
When others try to harm me or when I am surrounded by evil, thank you for being a secure dwelling place. Thank you for providing protection for me.

MY SHEPHERD
Just as you take care of the lilies of the field and the

birds in the air, you also care for me. Thank you for always watching over me.

A FRIEND THAT STICKS CLOSER THAN A BROTHER

God, thank you for always being there for me.

LILY OF THE VALLEY

Father, when I am in a low and dark place, the beauty of your presence surrounds me.

CHIEFEST OF TEN THOUSAND

Lord, no matter how many people I hold in high esteem, I put you in first place.

COUNSELOR

I'm grateful for therapists and counselors but you, O God, know me best. I know you have the best plan for my life.

ALTOGETHER LOVELY

God there is no blemish or flaw in you. Thank you for loving me despite my flaws.

PRINCE OF PEACE

You, Lord, speak peace, calm and tranquility to the storms that rage in my mind, my heart and in my life.

MY STRENGTH & MY SONG

You are my strength when I am weak. I will sing of your praises.

WONDERFUL

God everything you made is wonderful. I am fearfully and wonderfully made. Hallelujah!

THE ROCK OF AGES

God you are the same yesterday, today, and forever. You have proven yourself from generation to generation. I trust in you, my rock and my redeemer.

JEHOVAH-M'KADDESH

Lord, you are holy. Make me holy. Consecrate me for your service.

JEHOVAH-JIREH

God you are my provider. You are the one who supplies all of my needs.

JEHOVAH-NISSI

The Lord is my Banner! You wave your banner of love over me!

JEHOVAH-ROPHE

You are the Lord who heals. I am whole, in Jesus' name.

JEHOVAH-TSIDKENU

I am grateful for the blood you shed. Thank you for standing in the gap for me–making me blameless before God, for forgetting my sin.

JEHOVAH-SHALOM

God, you are my peace. Thank you that peace is my constant companion.

JEHOVAH-SHAMMAH

When others are nowhere to be found, I thank you for ALWAYS being there for me no matter when or why I'm calling.

I AM

When I'm hungry, you are bread. When I'm thirsty, you are living water. When I'm lonely, you are company. Whatever the need, great or small, you are!

ALPHA AND OMEGA

God, you are the beginning and the end. Help me to trust you in the middle.

MY DELIVERER

Whether from alcohol, drugs, fornication, gossip, lying, cheating–whatever my problem, THANK YOU for rescuing me and bringing me to the safety of your loving arms.

IMMANUEL

Because you are with me, I have nothing to fear.

MIGHTY GOD

I draw my strength, my confidence, and my boldness from you.

SAVIOUR

Dear Jesus, I come to you today and I repent of my sins. I believe you died for me. Please come into my heart. I want to make you my Lord and Savior. Amen!

LAMB OF GOD

Thank you for the sacrifice you made, carrying my sins away and nailing them to the cross.

ADONAI

You are God! You are Master of everything. We give praise unto you. We worship and adore you, O Holy One.

JEALOUS

I confess that at times I have put my time, talents, and tithes ahead of you. Forgive me for allowing others to take your place.

KING OF KINGS

I am a descendent of a Royal Priesthood. In all that I do and say, help me to always represent the kingdom of God well.

JESUS

Demons tremble. People are healed. Mountains are moved at the mention of your name! JESUS!

Extended Activity

What are other names of God?

_____

_____

_____

_____

_____

_____

_____

_____

_____

_____

Continue to explore the name, nature, and character of God to deepen and enrich your prayer life.

FIVE FINGER PRAYER

The Five Finger Prayer is a great way to teach children how to pray. To add creativity and fun, children can trace their hand then use different colors or draw faces on each finger; create finger puppets, or make a prayer collage.

Your Thumb
Pray for those closest to you (i.e. your loved ones, extended family, close friends).

Pointing Finger
Pray for those who teach, instruct, and heal (i.e. doctors, ministers and teachers).

Tallest Finger
Pray for our leaders (i.e. the president, education administrators, corporations).

Ring Finger
Pray for those who are weak, in trouble, or in pain. Pray for the lost (i.e. persons in hospitals, incarcerated persons, human trafficking and domestic violence victims, substance abusers).

Little Finger/Pinky
Pray for yourself.

SCRIPTURE SHOWERS

I was excited to learn that my church would begin offering a weekly prayer service. I shared my excitement with Rev. Deborah Richardson, who was the prayer leader at the time. When she extended the invitation for me to join the team, I was initially nervous and intimidated by the idea of planning, leading, and praying in a prayer service. She would often lead an exercise called *Scripture Showers*. All of the participants would have to find a scripture in the Bible, state the reference, and then read the text aloud. The exercise created an opportunity for everyone to participate in the service.

That exercise helped me to not only dig deeper into God's word, but it also helped me build my prayer life. Repeating God's word back to Him is a form of prayer. It helps when you are at a loss for words.

Below are a few of the scriptures we read aloud during those prayer services. Don't keep them to yourself. Gather your family, friends, or church members and share in God's word through *Scripture Showers*.

After reading, think about which of the scriptures resonate within your heart and spirit.

How does each scripture apply to your current situation or circumstance?

Scripture Showers

2 Corinthians 10:4-5

1 John 5:14-15

Proverbs 3:5

1 John 1:9

Psalm 32:8

John 8:31-2

1 Corinthians 10:13

Isaiah 43:2

Deuteronomy 30:19

Isaiah 55:11 3

Proverbs 16:3

Philippians 4:7-8

1 Corinthians 2:16

Psalm 34:19

Ephesians 4:31-32

Revelation 21:7-8

Proverbs 1:5

1 Corinthians 14:33

Hebrews 4:14-16

Psalm 42:5

Romans 8:28

Proverbs 3:5

Matthew 6:28-30

Job 23:28

Psalm 46:10

Philippians 1:6

Psalm 139:23-4

Romans 12:2

Jeremiah 29:11-13

Mark 4:24

Zechariah 4:6

Nehemiah 8:10

Joshua 1:8

John 2

Philippians 2:5

2 Timothy 1:7

Isaiah 26:3

Isaiah 53:5

Proverbs 18:10

Psalm 56:11

Ephesians 2:1-10

Mark 4:24

Romans 8:1

Proverbs 23:7

Isaiah 30:18

Romans 15:13

Romans 12:3

Extended Activity

Go back through the list. Read each scripture in different versions (ex. Easy Read Version, New Living Translation, New King James Version, The Message, Amplified, New International Version etc.).

What message is God communicating to you through His word about your situation or circumstance?

How will you practically apply the instructions God spoke to you through His word in your everyday living? Your prayer life?

PRAYER LETTER WRITING

Writing can be used as a tool to share our hearts with others. When devastating events occur, we may not be able to physically or financially support the persons effected or be able to participate in the relief efforts. Prayer letter writing is an opportunity to share God's love with others. Take the time to write a prayer. Send your written prayer by snail mail. Think about how nice will it be for someone to receive a love letter from God, written by you!

1. Think about the recipient of your letter.
2. Ask God for direction about the words to share in your prayer letter.
3. Share a scripture.
4. Encourage the recipient to pray for someone else.

Extended Activity: Create short prayers and send via email, text, or social media.

LORD, THIS IS HARD

"O Lord, I am calling to you. Please hurry! Listen when I cry to you for help! Accept my prayer as incense offered to you, and my upraised hands as an evening offering."

—Psalms 141:1-2 NLT

I CAN'T...

There are times when it is difficult to pray. Thank God that when our faith waivers, or we are bombarded by satanic attacks, when our hearts are overwhelmed and we cannot seem to find the words to pray, God provides.

Read and reflect on each of the following scriptures:

Luke 22:31-32 (Jesus)
Ephesians 1:17-19
Romans 8:26-27 (Holy Spirit)

TEARS ARE PRAYERS, TOO

Scripture Reflection: *Psalm 42*

Sometimes there are no words that can express the space our mind, heart, and/or spirit occupy. Our tears tell the story for us. Don't grab a tissue.

Allow the tears to come, to fall, to cleanse.

AMEN!

THE WAITING CLOSET

I bend my knees and the floor reaches up to support them.

Gently I lean my forehead upon my knotted hands and close my eyes.

I sigh…I wait. I wonder if today the cycle of silence will be broken.

The tick-tock of time passing thunders within my emptiness—

I am ready to give up. I feel like letting go.

Patience is slipping through my now loosely-clutched hands.

I wait, even though my knees are buckling underneath me—

Even though I don't feel like it anymore, I wait.

I can't hear anything, but I wait.

Everything within me wants to scream, yell, holler in despair.

God, where are you?

There are moments in our lives when we feel as though God is farthest from us. We wonder if He hears our prayers, senses our thoughts afar off, and sees our tears. In those moments when it feels like our prayers are not getting through, it is difficult to trust that He will ever answer. I encourage you to exercise a little faith. Don't give up! Instead, *"Wait on the Lord: be of good courage, and he shall strengthen thine heart: Wait, I say, on the Lord"* (Psalm 27:14). Know that while you are waiting on God, He already knows what you need and has already worked out the situation, problem, or circumstance.

Directions: Answer the following questions.

What are you waiting on God to do? To say?

How are you waiting on God to respond?

What are you doing in the wait-time?

What is your plan if the matter is not resolved or resolved in the manner you prayed or hoped?

HOLY SPIRIT, I WELCOME YOU

We do not have to face life's challenges on our own. The Holy Spirit is willing and able to lead, guide, and instruct us in handling every situation in our lives. Holy Spirit, you are welcome here!

Directions: Read each scripture. How can the Holy Spirit help you to persevere within your current situation?

Advocate (John 14:26)

Teacher (Luke 12:12)

Living Within (1 Corinthians 6:19)

Prayer Language/Communication (Acts 2:4)

HEALING SPIRIT:

To Build You Up (Jude 1:20)

To Give Us Power (Acts 1:8)

Do Not Grieve (Ephesians 4:30)

Do Not Resist (Acts 7:51)

MIGHTY SPIRIT:

Hope (Romans 15:13)

The Gift (1 Thessalonians 4:8)

Shaking (Acts 4:31)

Sit on Us (Luke 3:22)

Holy Spirit, have your way.
In Jesus' name I pray, Amen!

LAY ASIDE EVERY WEIGHT

"Therefore, since we are surrounded by so great a cloud of witnesses [who by faith have testified to the truth of God's absolute faithfulness], stripping off every unnecessary weight and the sin which so easily and cleverly entangles us, let us run with endurance and active persistence the race that is set before us ²[looking away from all that will distract us and] focusing our eyes on Jesus, who is the Author and Perfecter of faith [the first incentive for our belief and the One who brings our faith to maturity], who for the joy [of accomplishing the goal] set before Him endured the cross, disregarding the shame, and sat down at the right hand of the throne of God [revealing His deity, His authority, and the completion of His work]. Hebrews 12:1-2 (AMP)

Scripture Reflection:
Highlight, circle or underline words/phrases that stand out for you.

Because it is often difficult to feel, see, or notice spiritual weight gain, we don't realize that our pace during the faith race has slowed to a halt. Though use of Ecclesiastes 9:11 "…the race is not given to the swift…" is a justifiable excuse, when you are too heavy to run at all, you cease to participate in the race. You become a spectator and spectators don't reach the finish line nor do they obtain the prize. That's the enemy's goal, to weigh you down so you never get what God has in store for you.

What emotional, physical, and mental *things* are hindering your movement and causing you to stand still?

What sin (people, places, memories, situations, unforgiveness, bitterness, anger) is keeping you from LIVING the abundant life?

When people desire to lose weight, they often say it's best done with a partner. Prayer partners hold one another accountable. Who can help you run your Christian race in a manner that pleases God and helps you fulfill God's purpose for your life?

Whether you have a person (or people) you can trust to pray with you or you put your trust in Jesus Christ alone, make a commitment to accomplish your goal(s) and lose the weight of sin!

FAST & PRAY

Fasting is personal. It is often a time of great reflection, contemplation, and spiritual development. When fasting, a person typically refrains from eating, drinking, or behaving in a certain manner for a specified amount of time. Fasting also means adding dedicated time to prayer, seeking wisdom, clarity or direction about matters of life through reading God's word, and worshipping God in song, dance, or silence.

Read the first chapter of Daniel in its entirety, then answer the following questions.

Is there someone in your life that has similar characteristics as King Nebuchadnezzar? (v.1-2)

_____

_____

_____

_____

_____

_____

_____

_____

_____

Have you ever encountered a power struggle? (v. 3) If so, what was your response?

_____

_____

_____

_____

_____

_____

_____

_____

_____

Think about a time when you were required to ignore or disassociate from your cultural norms, values or beliefs. (v. 4-11) How did God sustain you during those moments?

_____

_____

_____

_____

_____

_____

_____

_____

Do you think it was solely by eating the vegetables and drinking water for ten days that made Daniel and his three friends have a greater level of ability and wisdom? What other things do you think they included during their time of fasting? (v. 12-17)

_____

_____

_____

_____

_____

_____

_____

_____

_____

_____

_____

_____

Compare & Contrast moments when you have prayed for God's direction and obeyed versus moments when you went out on your own or followed the instructions of someone else.

When God calls you to fast, be sure to add prayer!

FAITH(ING) IT

What is faith? *It is the confident assurance that something we want is going to happen. It is the certainty that what we hope for is waiting for us, even though we cannot see it up ahead.* Hebrews 11:1 (TLB)

There's a popular saying, "Fake it until you make it." As Christians, we are called to believe that if we have asked of God according to His will, our request is going to become a reality in our lives. Even though we cannot always see it with our natural eyes and do not understand how it will happen, we believe it will happen in our hearts.

When we have asked for something in prayer and not received it, or the waiting period seems too long and arduous, it is tempting to give up on God and feel forgotten. Experience has taught me that there is no faking it with God. He requires real faith. The Bible tells us in Hebrews 11:6, "But without faith it is impossible to please Him, for he who comes to God must believe that He is, and that He is a rewarder of those who diligently seek Him." Not only does God require faith but the scripture advises that God rewards consistency.

THINK: What am I believing God will do?

QUESTION: What is my level of faith? Have I stopped believing God for His promise(s)?

REFLECT: James 1:2-4

_____

_____

_____

_____

_____

_____

_____

_____

_____

_____

_____

_____

_____

_____

_____

_____

_____

_____

_____

MY PRAYER FOR PERSEVERANCE

Directions: Complete each prayer prompt. Include your responses when you *pray* aloud.

Father, how can I be happy when I am facing…
What trial(s) or trouble(s) are you currently facing in your life?

and you are testing my…
Identify the area(s) in your life that God is trying to strengthen in the midst of your trial/trouble.

Even though I do not always understand why things happen, I thank you for teaching me …
How is God teaching you to handle trials and trouble when they show up in your life? What is the lesson God wants you to learn?

Help me to have faith in you and obey your instructions so I can…
What is the result of persevering?

In Jesus' name, Amen

PERSONIFIED PUNCTUATION

The rules of punctuation in text messages, tweets, instant or direct messages, and email are often broken, absent, or ignored in an effort to get the message out quickly. God doesn't take shortcuts in His communication with us. Make a commitment to observe and obey the punctuation rules! Pray? Pray. Pray!

Directions: For each of the punctuation marks below, identify the scripture reference. Answer the question that follows.

PERIOD (.) *Declarative*

Stand still and see the salvation of the Lord, which He will accomplish for you today.

Scripture Reference: _____

What is God commanding you to do?

COMMA (,) *Pause*

Wait on the Lord; Be of good courage, And He shall strengthen your heart. Wait, I say, On the Lord!

Scripture Reference: _____

Why are you in a hurry? What is the rush costing you?

EXCLAMATION POINT (!) *Exclaim*
I AM!

Scripture Reference: _____

What has God given you to rejoice or shout about today?

QUESTION MARK (?) *Question*
For what does it profit a man if he gains the whole world and loses his soul?

Scripture Reference: _____

What questions do you want God to answer? What is He asking of you?

ELLIPSIS (…) *Sentence trails off*
And your latter days will be greater than the former…

Scripture Reference: _____

I am letting go…

SEMI-COLON (;) *Brief stop*

For the vision is yet for the appointed time; It hastens toward the goal and it will not fail. Though it tarries, wait for it; For it will certainly come, it will not delay.

Scripture Reference: _____

Do you need a moment to rest? Do you have unfinished business that requires closure in order for you to move forward?

COLON (:) *Introduce*
Present your bodies as a living sacrifice, holy and acceptable to God.

Scripture Reference: _____

How will you prepare for the new thing(s) God plans to introduce in your life?

PARENTHESIS () *Enclose*
Hide me under the shadow of your almighty wings.

Scripture Reference: _____

Are you surrounded by the right people in this season of your life?

DASH (-) *Interrupt*
Who shall separate us from the love of Christ?

Scripture Reference: _____

Why has God interrupted your plans?

HYPHEN (-) *Connect*
I am the vine. You are the branches.

Scripture Reference: _____

How have you strengthened your connection to God in prayer?

APOSTROPHE (') *Possession*
You shall have dominion over the fish…birds…land.

Scripture Reference: _____

Are you being a good steward over what God has given you?

APOSTROPHE (') *Missing Letters*
Consider the Parable of the Lost Coin in Luke 15:7-9

Scripture Reference: _____

What is missing in your life?

APOSTROPHE (') *Unusual Plurals*

Lord how many times shall I forgive my brother/sister who has sinned against me? …but seventy-seven times.

Scripture Reference: _____

Examine areas of excess. What can you do to downsize?

QUOTATION MARKS ("") *Spoken word*
Simon Peter, "Who do you say, I am?"

Scripture Reference: _____

QUOTATION MARKS ("") *Spoken word*
Jesus said, "Lo, I am with you always, even unto the end of the earth."

Scripture Reference: _____

What has God spoken to you? Have you obeyed? What is hindering/propelling your obedience?

REACHING THE FINISH LINE...

"Not that I have already attained, or am already perfected; but I press on, that I may lay hold of that for which Christ Jesus has also laid hold of me. Brethren, I do not count myself to have apprehended; but one thing I do, forgetting those things which are behind and reaching forward to those things which are ahead, I press toward the goal for the prize of the upward call of God in Christ Jesus."
—Philippians 3:12-14 (NIV)

Letting go is not always an easy task. There is a sense of comfort, familiarity and safety in clinging to memories, people and things that are dear to us. There is also danger. In holding on, we leave no room to receive the new things God has for us. Letting go of emotional, mental and relational baggage creates space and room in our lives for God to fulfill His plan. Ultimately, we must reach for our individual and collective finish lines.

"...In spite of adversity" (2 Corinthians 4: 8)

What hardship(s) or pain(s) do you need to forget and let go of in order to reach your finish line?

"...Toward financial freedom" (Luke 6:38)

Review your finances. Pray. Create a budget. Stick to it.

"…To receive healing" (Matthew 9:20)

Are you healthy—mentally, emotionally, physically and relationally? Where can you make improvements?

"…To be free from sin" (Romans 6:22-23)

Repeating, replaying or rehearsing your mistakes, missteps and mishaps is unhealthy. Repent. Accept God's Forgiveness. Forgive yourself. Press on!

"…To move forward" (Philippians 3:12)

What is God calling you to do? What is *His* plan and purpose for your life? Pray.

Create an action plan, inclusive of tasks, deadlines and accountability partners to achieve your goals.

REFLECT, REJOICE, RENEW

My Past

REFLECT: What things, people, and/or places do you need to release?

"…Forgetting what is behind and straining toward what is ahead, I press on toward the goal to win the prize for which God has called me heavenward in Christ Jesus." (Philippians 3:13-14 NIV)

_____

_____

_____

_____

_____

_____

_____

REJOICE: Think about all that God *has done* for you.

"The LORD is my strength and my shield; My heart trusted in Him, and I am helped; Therefore, my heart greatly rejoices, And with my song I will praise Him." (Psalm 28:7 NKJV)

_____

_____

_____

_____

_____

_____

RENEW: Ask for forgiveness. Receive God's forgiveness. Walk in forgiveness.

"And forgive your people, who have sinned against you; forgive all the offenses they have committed against you, and cause their conquerors to show them mercy;" (1 Kings 8:50 NIV)

_____

_____

_____

_____

_____

_____

My Present/Future

REFLECT: What is God calling you to do? Where is God calling you to go? What does God want you to say? Who is He calling you to serve?

"For I know the plans I have for you," declares the LORD, "plans to prosper you and not to harm you, plans to give you hope and a future." (Jeremiah 29:11 NKJV)

_____

_____

_____

_____

_____

_____

_____

REJOICE: Think about all that God *is doing* in your life.

"And we know that for those who love God all things work together for good, for those who are called according to his purpose." (Romans 8:28 NIV)

_____

_____

_____

_____

_____

_____

_____

RENEW: How has being in relationship with God through prayer, praise and worship given you a fresh start?

But now put these things out of your life: anger, losing your temper, doing or saying things to hurt others, and saying shameful things. ⁹Don't lie to each other. You have taken off those old clothes—the person you once were and the bad things you did then. ¹⁰Now you are wearing a new life, a life that is new every day. You are growing in your understanding of the one who made you. You are becoming more and more like him. (Colossians 3:8-10 NIV)

_____

_____

_____

_____

_____

_____

Therefore, if anyone is in Christ, he is a new creation.
The old has passed away; behold, the new has come.
—2 Corinthians 5:17 NIV

I love you, Lord!
You are my strength.
The Lord is my Rock, my
fortress, my place of safety.
He is my God, the Rock I
run to for protection.
He is my shield; by his
power I am saved.
He is my hiding place high
in the hills.
I called to the Lord for help,
and he saved me from my
enemies!
He is worthy of my praise!

—Psalms 18:1-3

LORD, I NEED YOUR HELP

GOD WANTS YOUR PERMISSION

In the early part of 2017, I needed God. I needed Him to answer some questions and to give me clarity in the steps He wanted me to take versus the direction I wanted to go. I was wrestling with my thoughts, unsettled in my spirit, and growing increasingly anxious about how things would work out in the end. I needed peace.

While sitting at the breakfast table on a Saturday morning during a women's retreat, the retreat host and teacher, Rev. Gail Simmons, sat down and said, "God wants your permission." Before I could retort, "…but I said, *Yes* to God already," Rev. Gail gently informed, "Giving Him permission is different from a Yes." Throughout the day, I pondered our breakfast moment.

During the time of impartation, Rev. Simmons sang the hymn, "Come Ye Disconsolate," over me. The spirit revealed some hurt that I was dealing with from serving in ministry. The song felt like salve being gently massaged on the wounds of the past. My father died when I was ten years old. One of my best friends had committed suicide during our sophomore year in college. My grandmother, my heart and my first model of a prayer warrior, died a few years after I graduated from college. I indeed had a *wounded heart* that therapy had not completely healed.

I went back to the hotel room before the evening prayer service had ended to process and pray about all that had taken place throughout that day. In that moment, kneeling next to the bed, I finally understood *why* God wanted my permission. When I prayed, I would always ask that God *massage the wounds of my heart.* God was not interested in "massaging" the wounds. He wanted to remove the wounds altogether. While He could have just taken the pain away from me, God is a gentleman. He would never force me or go against my will. **It was my responsibility to let go of the offenses, the hurts, and the disappointments.** Letting go would free up space in my heart. So, I released. I gave God permission to take the wounds once and for all. For the first time in several years, I was FREE!

Have you ever been hurt? Offended? Disappointed? Reflect on your experiences.

How did you handle or manage the hurt, offense or disappointment?

What *wounds* do you need to give God permission to take away so you too may walk in His FREEDOM?

Are you ready to give God permission? If not, what is keeping you from doing so?

God loves you! Bring your wounded heart to Him in prayer.

_____

_____

_____

_____

_____

_____

_____

_____

_____

_____

_____

_____

_____

_____

_____

_____

_____

_____

_____

_____

Come, Ye Disconsolate

Come, ye disconsolate,
where'er ye languish;
Come to the mercy-seat,
fervently kneel;
Here bring your wounded
hearts, here tell your
anguish,
Earth has no sorrow that
heaven cannot heal.

—Thomas Moore 1816, 1824

THE PLACE WHERE GOD LIVES

"Bethel" *(Genesis 35:3 NIV)* is the house of God. It is the place where God lives. God desires to reside in your life, on your job, in your home, and in your heart. Does God have a place to call home in you? Commit yourself to a lifestyle of prayer, worship and walking in the ways of God. Be the place where God lives.

THE FOUNDATION & BASEMENT

Cement (Matthew 16:18) Father, when the ground beneath me cracks, squeaks, or bends, remind me that I can stand firmly in you and on your word.

Washing Machine (2 Kings 5:10) Father, wash me with the blood of your son, Jesus Christ, that I may be whole and free from sin.

Dryer (Matthew 12:43-45) Father, when I tumble out of your will, and I follow the lead of someone/something other than you, forgive me.

Furnace (Daniel 3:8-26) Purify me! Remove anything that will keep me from fulfilling your will, your purpose, your plan for my life.

Carpet/Furnishings (Exodus 36:1) Father, may I feel the weight of your glory as I lay prostrate before you.

THE HOUSE

Door (Hebrews 11:28) Lord, I welcome you into my life. Cover me and keep me safe. Show me who to allow in and to keep out of my life, I pray. Amen!

Window (Matthew 26:41) Lord, open the eyes of my understanding. Help me see your handiwork in everything and everywhere.

Kitchen (Romans 14:17) Lord, we thank you for being a provider; remind us to reach out to others with the same hands we lift up to you.

Bathroom (Isaiah 61:3b) Lord, send a spiritual refreshing in my life. Shower me with your love and bathe me in the sweet anointing of the Holy Spirit.

Bedroom (Isaiah 40:29) Lord, help me to surrender and find rest in you!

THE ATTIC/STORAGE

Roof (Psalm 91:9-11) Dad, with you, I am safe. In you, I can always find a hiding place.

Boxes (Luke 6:38) Dad, help me to let go of the past and welcome a new beginning.

Photograph Albums (Psalm 37:25) Dad, though some of my loved ones are now in heaven with you, I thank you for the memories.

Toys (Matthew 5:8) Dad, I am your child. Give me a pure heart, a joyful countenance and a trusting heart.

Dust (Psalm 104:27-28) Dad, when my work on earth is done, may you say, "Well done."

GOD WITHIN ME, GOD AROUND ME, GOD HOLDING ME

Such knowledge is too wonderful for me, too lofty for me to attain. Where can I go from your Spirit? Where can I flee from your presence? If I go up to the heavens, you are there; if I make my bed in the depths, you are there. Psalms 139:6-8

Sometimes we get in a hurry. Slow down! Focus your prayers on one scripture for the entire week. Use the prayer prompt or pray on your own. At the end of each week, reflect on God's message to you.

God Within Me

Using the following weekly prompts, create a list of the great things God has placed within you.

Week 1: Genesis 2:7

Prayer: God you formed me and breathed into me the breath of life. I exist because YOU gave me life.

Week 1: What is God's message to you?

_____

_____

_____
_____
_____
_____
_____

Week 2: Philippians 1:6

Prayer: Father when I lose confidence, remind me that it was YOU that began a great work in me and you are not through with me yet.

Week 2: What is God's message to you?

_____
_____
_____
_____
_____
_____

Week 3: Isaiah 59:21

Prayer: Lord, thank you for promising to not depart from me. Thank you for your word that allows me to speak life from generation to generation.

Week 3: What is God's message to you?

_____

_____

_____

_____

_____

_____

_____

Week 4: Ezekiel 37:14

Prayer: I declare that I shall live!

Week 4: What is God's message to you?

_____

_____

_____

_____

_____

_____

_____

Week 5: Psalm 51:10

Prayer: Create in me a pure and clean heart, O God.

Week 5: What is God's message to you?

_____

_____

_____

_____

_____

_____

_____

_____

God Around Me

Create a list describing how you know that God is near.

Week 1: Luke 12:24, 27

Prayer: Father, I look at all that you have created. All I have ever needed, your hand has provided.

Week 1: What is God's message to you?

_____

_____

_____

_____

_____

_____

_____

_____

_____

Week 2: Psalm 139:7

Prayer: Father it is useless trying to hide from you. Let me walk in the light of your love. Help me bring my darkness to you and ask for your tender mercy.

Week 2: What is God's message to you?

_____

_____

_____

_____

_____

_____

_____

_____

Week 3: Isaiah 54:17

Prayer: There are forces of darkness all around me but I give thanks, glory, honor, and praise to my Father who does not allow them to ever have victory over me.

Week 3: What is God's message to you?

_____

_____

_____

_____

_____

_____

_____

_____

Week 4: Psalm 23

Prayer: Thank you that wherever I may go, goodness and mercy follow me.

Week 4: What is God's message to you?

_____

_____

_____

_____

_____

_____

_____

_____

<u>God Holding Me</u>

When do you need to be held, comforted, and/or made to feel secure? Create a list.

Week 1: Psalm 145:14

Prayer: Dad, when I fall down, I am thankful that you pick me up, dust me off, and put me back in the place where you desire for me to stand.

Week 1: What is God's message to you?

_____

_____

_____

_____

_____

_____

_____

_____

Week 2: 2 Corinthians 1:3-4

Prayer: Father, I am comforted by your love. May the love you show me be reflected in my relationship with others.

Week 2: What is God's message to you?

_____

_____

_____

_____

_____

_____

_____

_____

Week 3: Isaiah 26:3

Prayer: In times of confusion, despair, pain and suffering, O Lord, grant me peace.

Week 3: What is God's message to you?

_____

_____

_____

_____

_____

_____

_____

_____

Week 4: Ruth 2:12

Prayer: You are my hiding place. There is safety in your bosom.

Week 4: What is God's message to you?

_____

_____

_____

_____

_____

_____

_____

Week 5: Jeremiah 18:6

Prayer: I am your clay. Mold, make, and shape me for your purpose.

Week 5: What is God's message to you?

_____

_____

_____

_____

_____

_____

WHOLE ARMOR OF GOD

The Armor of God is a spiritual wardrobe that consists of timeless pieces that never go out of style. So, why exactly do you need these items in your wardrobe? 1 Peter 5:8 warns us: *Your adversary the devil prowls around like a roaring lion, seeking someone to devour.*

The enemy looks for opportunities to catch us naked—off guard, off task, and out of focus. We need God's supernatural power to protect us from the ongoing attacks of Satan's army. In our most vulnerable moments, God provides an affordable, one-size-fits-all covering for His children. While it may not be featured on the fashion week runway, it is a must-have collection created by a one-of-a-kind designer. Order your armor today through prayer!

Directions: Create a list of your current battles/struggles. Use your five senses (sight, smell, sound, taste, touch) to describe the image of fighting your current battles/struggles in your *own* strength.

Read: Ephesians 6:10-20

Helmet:
We put on the helmet to protect our mind, eyes, ears and mouths.

Mind
Identify your thoughts. What type of thoughts try to penetrate your mind when your "helmet" is off? How can God's helmet protect you from Satan's attacks against your mind?

Eyes
What differences do you notice when you look through the eyes of faith versus seeing with your natural eyes? How is your vision? What is God's vison for your life?

Mouth
What are you saying to yourself? How has the enemy used your own words against you? How has he used the words of others?

_____

_____

_____

_____

_____

_____

_____

Prayer Focus: *Renewed focus, spiritual hearing, the mind of Christ, word choice, greater level of discernment.*

Breastplate:
We put on the breastplate of righteousness to guard our heart and lungs.

Have you ever experienced a loss of breath? In what areas of your life do you feel constrained or restricted? Have you asked God to breathe fresh life into that area of your life?

Sometimes we expose our hearts to the wrong persons. What has "damaged" your heart? Have you asked God to mend your heart?

_____

_____

_____

_____

_____

_____

_____

Prayer Focus: *Clean heart. Forgiveness. Fresh wind of God. Breath of God. Calm. Peace.*

Belt
We put on the belt that securely buckles at the waist. God holds us up with His strength and holds us accountable to His word. Satan is the father of lies.

There is no truth in him. Everything he says leads to death and destruction. Jesus is *the way, and the truth, and the life.* (John 14:6).

Directions: Fold a piece of paper in half down the center. On the left side of the folded paper, write a list of lies. Things you may have said to yourself or things others may have said about you that are not true. Next to each lie, on the right side of the paper, write statements of truth found in scripture. Then, discard, the left side of the paper.

Focus on the God's TRUTH about you!

Prayer Focus: *Clarity. Truth. Justice. Connection. Unity. Wisdom. Knowledge. Understanding.*

Shoes
We put on the shoes. Shoes help us to stand on the promises and truth of God's word. Shoes, like people, can become worn and in need of repair. Think about your prayer life.

How is your prayer life in relation to the condition of your shoes? Which one is in better shape—your shoes or your prayer life? What is your plan?

_____

_____

_____

_____

_____

_____

_____

_____

_____

_____

Prayer Focus: _Strength. Courage. Deep roots in Christ. Bear fruit. Guidance. God's will._

Sword & Shield

We carry the sword (God's word) in one hand. We lift up the shield with the other hand. God's word penetrates and destroys the plans, tricks and schemes of the enemy. Exercising our faith causes the shield to grow. Lifting it up stops the tactics of the enemy from ever succeeding.

Imagine yourself in a fight with the enemy. Who is currently winning? What tactics are being used in the fight? What scriptures will you use to defeat him?

How can prayer assist in the development of your faith? List persons who can assist you defeating the enemy by faith.

Prayer Focus: *Faith. Fruit of the Spirit (Galatians 5:22).*

_____

_____

_____

_____

_____

_____

_____

_____

_____

_____

_____

_____

_____

_____

_____

_____

_____

_____

_____

_____

_____

_____

_____

PULLING DOWN STRONGHOLDS

Strong. Hold. Think about when someone holds you tightly. It is hard to break free or get out of the person's grip without exerting strong force.

Freedom from strongholds requires breakthrough!

Directions: Answer the questions and complete the breakthrough action steps. Read and reflect on God's message to you within the scripture reading.

"But I am afraid that your minds will be led away from your true and pure following of Christ. This could happen just as Eve was tricked by that snake with his clever lies."
2 Corinthians 11:3 ERV

In a message that my former Sunday School teacher, Sheerene Brown, preached, she suggested screaming a hearty and loud, "Shut Up, Satan!" when he gets in your ear and overwhelms your mind. I've used it often as an initial step to bring peace to my mind.

What is the weakness, negative mindset or bad habit that Satan enjoys boxing you in and beating you over the head with repeatedly?

_____

_____

_____

_____

_____

_____

_____

_____

Breakthrough Action Step 1:
Exclaim, "SHUT UP, Satan!"

Can anything separate us form Christ's love? Can trouble or problems or persecution separate us from his love? If we have no food or clothes or face danger or even death, will that separate us from his love?" Romans 8:35 ERV

Satan wants to separate you from God. He wants to make you believe that God does not want or love you because of your secret, habit, or weakness. The scripture tells us that NO THING (nothing) can separate us from God's love.

What has Satan told you to keep as a secret from God?

_____

_____

_____

_____

_____

_____

_____

_____

Breakthrough Action Step 2:
FORGIVE. Forgive yourself. Ask for, accept, and
receive forgiveness from God.

For we do not wrestle against flesh and blood, but against the rulers, against the authorities, against the cosmic powers over this present darkness, against the spiritual forces of evil in the heavenly places. Ephesians 6:12 ESV

Name a specific stronghold (secret, habit, weakness) you are bringing to God in prayer: *If you have more than one, bring each one to God separately.*

_____

_____

_____

_____

_____

_____

_____

_____

Breakthrough Action Step 3:
CONFESS. Ask God to deliver you from the
stronghold.

We live in this world, but we don't fight our battles in the same way the world does. ⁴The weapons we use are not human ones. Our weapons have power from God and can destroy the enemy's strong places. We destroy people's arguments, ⁵and we tear down every proud idea that raises itself against the knowledge of God. We also capture every thought and make it give up and obey Christ. 2 Corinthians 10:3-5 ERV

Human nature causes us to think we must fight with a fist, weapon or substance, or fight with money, influence and power. The Bible, however, teaches us that the weapons God provides help us fight in the spirit realm and WIN!

Have you been in a fight lately? Which method did you use to fight? What was the outcome?

Compare and contrast the world versus God's method of fighting. Think about who may have been negatively impacted by your actions. What relationships may need to be repaired?

What is God instructing you to do?

_____

_____

_____

_____

_____

_____

_____

Breakthrough Action Step 4:
CHANGE your behavior.

So, I tell you, live the way the Spirit leads you. Then you will not do the evil things your sinful self wants. [17] The sinful self wants what is against the Spirit, and the Spirit wants what is against the sinful self. They are always fighting against each other, so that you don't do what you really want to do. [18] But if you let the Spirit lead you, you are not under law.

[19] The wrong things the sinful self does are clear: committing sexual sin, being morally bad, doing all kinds of shameful things, [20] worshiping false gods, taking part in witchcraft, hating people, causing trouble, being jealous, angry or selfish, causing people to argue and divide into separate groups, [21] being filled with envy, getting drunk, having wild parties, and doing other things like this. I

warn you now as I warned you before: The people who do these things will not have a part in God's kingdom. Galatians 5:16-21 ERV

Take inventory of your lifestyle. What is God's message to you?

What are His instructions for improvement?

_____

_____

_____

_____

_____

_____

_____

_____

Breakthrough Action Step 5:
CHECK-IN. Before you enter the ring, always check in with God!

KILLING GOLIATH

READ: 1 Samuel 17

Every person encounters some type of "giant" on a daily basis. The list below represents examples of the issues, problems, and circumstances that threaten to kill or destroy us. **Use the power God gives us through prayer to take these giants down.** Remember, God is BIGGER, and with His help, we can conquer every Goliath we encounter!

DIRECTIONS: Identify the giant you are currently facing. Reflect upon what the giant says to you. How does the giant make you feel? What tools do you have to defeat the giant? Remember, God has already won the battle. Check in with Him for the battle plan in prayer.

POTENTIAL GIANTS

FEAR	LOW SELF ESTEEM
ANGER	CANCER
GENERATIONAL CURSES	OBESITY
	WAR
DIVORCE	ALCOHOLISM
MENTAL ILLNESS	POVERTY
RACISM	WORRY
LACK	AIDS
DEATH & LOSS	HATRED
UNFORGIVENESS	HIGH BLOOD PRESSURE
HOMELESSNESS	HOPELESSNESS
DIABETES	UNEMPLOYMENT
HUNGER	ABANDONMENT
CONFUSION	OTHER:
COVID-19	_____
	_____

Extended Activity

What does the Bible say about each of the issues in the list above? How did persons in the Bible handle these situations? What prayers did they pray? Search the scripture to find the answers.

THIS IS MY CONFESSION

Father, in the name of Jesus, I boldly confess your word over my life. I declare that from this day forward, I will walk the steps you have ordered for my life—fulfilling the plan, the purpose and the destiny you designed just for me.

I Confess....

Evening and morning and at noon, I will come boldly unto the throne of grace to obtain mercy and find grace to help in my time of need.

I will not fear because you have not given me a spirit of fear, but of power, love and a sound mind.

I have the mind of Christ.

Greater is He that is within me than he that is in the world.

There is NO weapon formed against me that shall prosper.

I will commit my works to you, Lord, and my thoughts will be established.

I will prosper and be in good health, even as my soul prospers.

You can search me, O God, and know my heart; try me, and know my thoughts:

When I'm impatient, I will trust in you with all my heart and lean not to my own understanding. I will wait on you and be of good courage.

When I'm anxious, I will be still and know that you are God.

When I lack confidence, I will remember that I am fearfully and wonderfully made, the head and not the tail, above and not beneath; a lender and not a borrower.

It is because of you that:
I am blessed! HALLELUJIAH!
I am healed! HALLELUJIAH!
I am whole! HALLELUJIAH!
I am victorious! HALLELUJIAH!
I am free! HALLELUJIAH!
HALLELUJIAH!
HALLELUJIAH!
HALLELUJIAH!

LORD, HEAR MY PRAYERS

"I urge, then, first of all, that petitions, prayers, intercession and thanksgiving be made for all people—"

—1 Timothy 2:1

A PRAYER FOR YOU

May God grant you wisdom beyond your years.

May God use your eyes as a screen to project His vision for your life.

May God whisper in your ears sentiments of His never-ending love for you.

May God's presence be a sweet-smelling fragrance dancing through your nostrils.

May God's heart smile because of the worship and praise that pour endlessly from your lips.

May God's hands catch the heavy burdens before they fall onto your shoulders.

May God choose your hands to further build His Kingdom.

May God be permitted to remove the hurt and pain hidden deep in your heart.

May God give you a greater capacity for forgiveness.

May God breathe into your lungs a fresh wind of peace that soothes your soul.

May God show you how to walk with authority and to possess everything He has already promised you.

May God always smile because He sees His reflection in you!

PRAYER FOR PASTORS & LEADERS

Hallelujah! Hallelujah! Hallelujah! We, your people, come before you to stand in agreement, to empower, to encourage and to support the vision and the visionary of this church. God, we thank you for his/her life and for their family. We ask that you would touch him/her from the crown of their head to the very soles of their feet.

Touch his/her mind: give him/her wisdom and understanding beyond their years. We bind the enemy in the area of confusion and we rebuke a double-minded spirit. Give him/her peace. Give him/her focus that he/she may lead this church, their family, and the lost in a closer walk and relationship with you.

Touch his/her eyes: cause him/her to see what you see. Remove the scales from his/her eyes. Take away anything that would hinder him/her from seeing the vision clearly. Grant him/her razor-sharp discernment. Cause him/her to have supernatural vision. Show him/her the strategies that he/she needs to confuse, escape, and defeat the enemy.

Touch his/her ears: cause him/her to hear every word that proceeds from your lips. Oh God, in his/her midnight hour, when he/she doesn't know which way to turn, cause him/her to be still and listen for your tender voice. Then Oh God, cause him/her to obey the instructions, to follow the orders, and to carry out the assignment as you have given it to him/her. And when he/she dares to turn left or right, ignoring your voice and trying to go his/her own way, Holy Spirit arrest him/her and place him/her back on the right path.

Touch his/her lips: may his/her words be seasoned with grace. Give him/her to know when to speak and when to be quiet. May he/she be your mouthpiece and speak what thus saith the Lord.

Touch his/her shoulders: remove every weight that would hinder his/her ability to walk tall in you God.

Touch his/her heart: help him/her to let go of every hurt, every set back, and every disappointment. Oh God, help him/her to forgive and to receive your forgiveness. Hide your word in his/her heart so that in the days when he/she feels alone and misunderstood, your word will rise up, encourage and restore their strength.

Touch his/her lungs: when he/she feels like giving up and throwing in the towel, breathe into him/her the breath of life that he/she may continue running the race to see what the end will be.

Touch his/her hands: may the works of his/her hands be productive and blessed. Cause him/her to never be ashamed to lift their hands in worship and adoration unto you. And with those same hands, Oh God, give him/her the desire to reach them out to help the poor, to heal the sick, and to befriend the friendless.

Touch his/her knees: Oh God, that he/she may spend time on bended knee, seeking your face and basking in your presence. For in your presence there is fullness of joy and at your right hand there are pleasures forever more.

Touch his/her feet: may he/she walk out the steps that have been ordered, purposed, and destined for his/her life. Enlarge their territory and give him/her to walk in the authority and power that you've given him/her. May his/her ministry trample upon and bruise the head of the enemy. May he/she always keep pace with you.

Cover him/her with the blood of your son, Jesus Christ. Cause your angels to keep watch over him/her and encamp around him/her both day and night. And when his/her journey is over, may you say, "Well done my good and faithful servant."

This is our prayer and we ask that it be so, in Jesus' name, Amen! Amen! Amen!

PRAYER FOR WOMEN IN MINISTRY

*Below is a text message I sent to women I
served in ministry with a few years ago.*

During my prayer time this morning, I asked that God
would keep us in step with Him; don't allow us to
misstep but to stay in pace with Him during this
season. To stay in tune to the very words that fall from
His lips. To seek His face and sit at His feet until He
shows us our next move, gives us our next assignment.
That He would align us to His will and unite His
kingdom.

That He would enlarge our capacity, our territory
and position us so that His power and His glory would
be seen throughout earth. That we would trust Him
when we can't trace Him, clench to His unfailing hand
and hold fast to our faith that He is our God and our
trust, hope and joy are in Him alone.

This is our new season and we sit in great
anticipation and expectation of what our Father will do
for, in, and through His daughters. Amen!

This is the prayer I prayed that morning:

Father, we thank you that in this season, you are
masterfully and strategically opening new doors and

assigning your children to do great things for your glory.

Holy Spirit, we welcome you to rest, reign, rule and abide within us. Search us, cleanse us, make us ever ready to serve at your pleasure.

We decree and declare a new season where our gift(s) will make room for us and usher us into the presence of great men/women. We decree and declare that our latter days shall be greater than our former days.

We believe you are the only wise God, who is able to do the exceedingly, abundantly above all in our lives and in the lives of those that are genuinely connected to us.

Father, stir up the gift(s). Cause your love-light to shine in and through us. Let the world see you in all we do.

We decree and declare that you are Jehovah Rapha, the God that heals our diseases. Jehovah Shalom, the God that brings peace to our minds, hearts, spirit and situations.

We decree and declare that you are the author and finisher of our faith and that the plans you have for us are good. So, we fix our eyes on you. We ask for your wisdom, a greater level of discernment and your word to light our pathway.

We make a conscious choice to commit our ways to you and to surrender our will into your most capable hands.

Increase our faith. Build our fervor for the assignment you've given us. Set our hearts on fire for you, God!

When all is said and done, we will be careful to give ALL honor, glory, and praise to YOU because you deserve and are so worthy of it. In Jesus' name, Amen!

PRAYER FOR GRIEF, LOSS & HEALING

Father, I come to you on behalf of those who have lost loved ones, on behalf of those who may need healing, and on behalf of those who are at a loss for what to do next. God, all is dark and we cannot seem to find our way into your light. I pray you will overwhelm us with your warm and loving embrace. Remind us that you are near to the broken-hearted. You are Jehovah Rapha, the God who heals us. Our hope is in you. Our trust is in you. You are the only one that can heal us from our disease. Thank you for those you send to stand in the gap. Thank you for your angels that keep watch over us.

May the blood of Jesus cover your people. I come against the spirits of loneliness, giving up, and feeling hopeless. I come against worry and fear about what tomorrow may bring. I come against division and strife among family members. I declare that your people walk in peace knowing you will supply all of their needs. Cause your people not to be afraid because you have already gone ahead and you work all things together for the good. Thank you, Jesus, Amen.

Read/Reflect Scriptures

Isaiah 40:18-31   *Psalm 55:22*

Isaiah 49:16   *Isaiah 51:3*

John 14:1-4   *Matthew 5:4*

Nahum 1:7   *Matthew 11:25-30*

Romans 8:31-39   *2 Corinthians 1:3-5*

Philippians 4:6   *Hebrews 4:14-16*

1 Peter 5:6-7   *Revelation 21:4*

PRAYER FOR BATTLING DEPRESSION/ANXIETY/SUICIDE IDEATION

God, you said you would never leave or forsake me. I need you right now. Send divine light to illuminate every dark space within me. Silence the raging and distorting thoughts that are overwhelming my mind. Drown out every negative voice whispering in my ears. Show me a way out of this pain. Give me peace. I praise you in advance!

I REBUKE YOU SATAN! I DO NOT BELONG TO YOU! I PLEA THE BLOOD OF JESUS OVER MY MIND! I TAKE AUTHORITY OVER MY MIND AND MY EMOTIONS! I COMMAND MY MIND AND MY EMOTIONS TO COME IN ALIGNMENT WITH GOD'S WORD AND GOD'S WILL FOR MY LIFE!

According to the word of God, I will not die, but live and declare the works of the Lord. I decree and declare that I am transformed by the entire renewal of my mind. I decree and declare that I think on those things that are just, pure, lovely, kind and true. I decree and declare that I have a sound mind. I decree and declare that the God of peace is my companion. I praise you Lord. You have a plan for me that is good! I will live! In Jesus' mighty name, Amen!

PRAYER OF HEALING FOR COVID-19 VICTIMS

Abba Father, Sovereign God, we come humbly into your presence asking that you hear our earnest plea to bring TOTAL healing and restoration to *(person's name)*'s body.

We decree and declare that you are able to do exceedingly and abundantly above all we can ask, think, or imagine. Dispatch your angels to *(hospital name or location)*. We decree and declare that *(person's name)*'s body will come into divine alignment according to your will, your purpose and your plan. Thank you that *(person's name)* is covered and protected under the blood of Jesus Christ.

We know you to be our Jehovah Rapha, the God who heals. We know you to be Jehovah Shalom, the God of our peace. Show forth your mighty hand and let your healing virtue flow NOW, in the name of Jesus.

Touch and grant Godly wisdom, knowledge and understanding to every person that will come in contact with *(person's name)*. Holy Spirit, Comforter, be with *(person's name)*'s family and friends. Lift the burdens of worry, anxiety and fear. Help them find confidence in knowing that *(person's name)* is in your most capable hands.

We thank you that we shall hear testimony of your miracles, signs and wonders in the days ahead. We declare VICTORY in advance! Your will be done! When all is said and done, we will be careful to give you Lord, all the glory, honor and praise. We ask all these things in Jesus' name. Amen, Amen, Amen!

PRAYER FOR
ENGAGEMENT/MARRIAGE

Father, we thank you that perfect love casts out all fear. Because you, O God, are love, we have assurance in those that you bring into our lives to manifest your love in our lives. I pray God, you will seal this engagement/marriage in your son's precious blood. Cover the couple. Keep them and direct them. May they hear from you in this season, clearly and without distortion, like never before.

We thank you that no weapon that forms against them or the covenant they will make/have made with you, will prosper. Every attack, plot and scheme of the enemy is cancelled and cursed at the root. The blood of Jesus stands against every attack.

Thank you for the angels that will keep watch over them both day and night. May their love, ministry and purpose be entwined in your triune love, will and purpose. We declare and we decree it to be so. In Jesus' name, AMEN!

PRAYER FOR THE FAMILY

Our Father and our God, we pray you will give parents the wisdom, knowledge, desire, and love to raise their children in a God-like manner and in the fear of the Lord. Thank you, Father, that you perfect that which concerns mothers and fathers, guardians and caretakers. Help them to commit to prayer and not to faint, lose heart, or give up. As they draw boldly near the throne of grace, may they receive mercy and find grace to help in their time of need.

Father, help parents train up their children in the way they should go, so when they are old, they will not depart from you. God you said, if we ask anything according to your will, you hear us; and if we know that you hear us, whatsoever we ask, we know that we have the petitions that we desired of you.

Thank you that our children are the head and not the tail. We pray, God, that you will save our children and youth for they are gifts from you. Help them obey your voice and to cling to you for God, you are their life and the length of their days. We pray your angels take charge over our children and provide them with divine protection. God, keep them safe and covered under the blood of Jesus. Guide them in making the right choices throughout life. Fill them with the knowledge of your will and cause them to bear fruit in every good work.

May they find favor, good understanding, and high esteem in your sight and in the sight of their teachers, professors and employers. Help our children to trust you, to find their refuge in you and to stand rooted and grounded in your love.

God, you said you word will not return unto you void, but will accomplish what it says it will do. Therefore, we believe in the name of Jesus that all the needs of the family are met, according to your riches in glory. Lord God, may your divine power give every family everything they need. Thank you that the Holy Spirit is welcome and resides in their homes. Thank you for blessing their homes and rebuking the devourer. Thank you that we will not eat the bread of idleness, gossip, discontent and self-pity.

We declare on the authority of your word that our families will be mighty in the land and that wealth and riches are in our houses. We commit this prayer unto you God. We trust and believe you will cause the thoughts of every parent, guardian, caretaker and child to become in agreement to your will so their plans may be established and succeed. In Jesus' name we pray, Amen!

A PRAYER FOR GRADUATES

Father, in the name of Jesus, I thank you because I'm fearfully and wonderfully made. Before I was even born, you created a plan for my life. You have been with me in my mountaintop experiences and you have been with me during my valley lows. Today, I stand as proof that I have stayed the course. I have studied to show myself approved and I have passed the tests.

As I turn my tassel, I turn to new chapters in my life, new levels to aspire to, and new responsibilities to assume. I commit to daily becoming who you have called, predestined and purposed me to be on earth. Today God, I take comfort in knowing there is no place along this new leg of my journey where I am alone. I am empowered by your word that says, "I can do ALL things because you give me strength." I vow today, that in all my ways, my thoughts, my desires, my plans, I will acknowledge you and by faith, I know you will forever direct my path.

I thank you because it is you that gives me the courage I need to leave a space that has become so familiar. I take firm hold of your unchanging hands as I embark on new career paths and seek higher levels of education. As I walk the steps you have ordered, fulfilling the vision and chasing the divine dream, Holy Spirit, please be my guide!

And when the way gets rough and I feel like giving up, I ask that you let your grace carry me through, over, and around every obstacle. When the weight of the world feels like it will crush me, let the power of your son's blood revive, renew, and sustain me until my victory comes! When I face rejection, remind me that the Greater One lives inside me! When the vision seems to tarry, help me wait on you and be of good courage! When I'm in doubt and I hang my head, be the lifter of my head and grant me the peace that surpasses all understanding! When I worry or am afraid, be my wonderful counselor and grant me the power, love, and sound mind that conquers fear and chases doubt away! When I'm lonely, be the friend that sticks closer than a brother!

Be the I AM GOD as I take my rightful place and get in my predestined position. Today, Most Holy God, I commit myself to you. Bless the work of my hands so when I meet you in glory, you will say, "Well Done!" This is my prayer, and I ask it in the matchless name of Jesus the Christ! Amen! Amen! Amen!

WE COME

We come seeking God's face.

We come surrendering our hearts, our minds, our souls, our wills, our plans.

We come to offer ourselves as a living sacrifice.

We want to be holy.

We want our worship and our lives to be acceptable unto you, God.

We come with a spirit of expectation and in anticipation of a move by you.

We come crying out, "It's me, it's me, it's me O Lord standing in the need of prayer!"

We come to raise our voices and birth a sound of worship unto you like never before.

We come as open vessels with a desire to be filled with your fresh anointing, your power, your love.

We come with all that we are.

We come to give ourselves to you Lord.

Mold
Make
Change
Rearrange
Shake up
Uproot
Transition
Provide
Heal
Set Free
Save
Deliver
Break
Reshape
Dry up
Press
Squeeze
Open
Move out
Enlarge
Flow
Touch
Breathe –

Do whatever. However. Whenever and through whomever.

We invite you to inhabit our praise.

We welcome you into the sanctuary of our hearts.

Dwell among us.

Don't leave us!

Don't let us go until you accomplish what you plan to do, in us..

With us…

And through us.

We come open and ready to receive your deposit.

We come.

AMEN!

Acknowledgments

Thank you, Lord, for being patient with me. There were so many times when I stopped working on this project because I was afraid of what others would say and think. I have come to finally realize that what you think of me is all that really matters. Thank you that nothing goes to waste. It has all been for my good.

To my grandmother, Shirley Plant, who I miss so very much. Nanny...Sunshine, you were the first prayer warrior I knew. I watched you and Lorraine Taylor (Aunt Jewel), and Lucille Moore (Ma Moore) have prayer and devotional service from your homes. You ladies were my first example. *Elder Lisa Barber,* you will always hold a special place in my heart. Your intimacy with God was evident in the way you prayed to "Daddy God." Though you all rest in heaven now, I believe your spirit is with me even as I type these words.

To my mom, Geneva Morrison, who reminds me to "Wait on the Lord" and to "Hold to His Unchanging Hands," thank you for always being there and listening to me. For your hugs and your quiet patience and faith, I love and appreciate you always.

To my little tall sister, April Morrison, you know just how to brighten my days in moments when I feel as though my faith has run out and my self-esteem has hit rock bottom. Love you to life.

To my aunt, RoseAnn Martin, thank you for your continued encouragement and my cousins for all the laughs and support.

To Bernice Holmes, Marcia Howard, Deborah Richardson, Teora Summers, and Ronda Littleton-Johnson, thank you for welcoming me into your homes. Those intimate moments of sharing and prayer have changed my life for the better.

To everyone who I have had the honor and privilege to pray with and to pray for through the years, thank you for trusting the God in me. I pray those moments drew you closer to Him!

To you, you and you....

"The Lord bless you
and keep you;
the Lord make his face shine on you
and be gracious to you;
the Lord turn his face toward you
and give you peace."

Numbers 6:24-26